Let's Explore

My day

by Henry Pluckrose

W

FRANKLIN WATTS
NEW YORK • LONDON • SYDNEY

Author's note

This book is one of a series which has been designed to encourage young readers to think about the everyday concepts that form part of their world. The text and photographs complement each other, and both elements combine to provide starting points for discussion. Although each book is complete in itself, each title links closely with others in the set, so presenting an ideal platform for learning.

I have consciously avoided 'writing down' to my readers. Young children like to know the 'real' words for things, and are better able to express themselves when they can use correct terms with confidence.

Young children learn from the experiences they share with adults around them. The child offers his or her ideas which are then developed and extended through the adult. The books in this series are a means for the child and adult to share informal talk, photographs and text, and the ideas which accompany them.

One particular element merits comment. Information books are also reading books. Like a successful story book, an effective information book will be turned to again and again. As children develop, their appreciation of the significance of fact develops too. The young child who asks 'Why do we need clocks?' may subsequently and more provocatively ask, 'Who invented time?' Thoughts take time to generate. Hopefully books like those in this series provide the momentum for this.

Henry Pluckrose

Contents

Still asleep?
It's morning and time to get up!
What will you do
with your time today?

It's time to get washed and dressed.
What clothes will you wear today?

It's breakfast time.
What things do you like
to eat for breakfast?

10

It's important to remember to brush your teeth before you go to school.

It's time to leave for school.

Have you remembered everything?

Books, pencils and packed lunch?

If you get to school early,
there's time to play
before lessons begin.

Lessons fill up the day.

There's reading, writing and maths.

What else do you learn at school?

Then it's time for lunch.
And after lunch,
there's more time to play.

Sometimes, in the afternoon, there's a visit to the library. What kind of books do you like best?

School's over, it's time to go home.
But first, there's shopping
to get from the supermarket.

Home at last and it's time to play games and watch TV before you have tea.

It's bath time!

Do you like playing in the water?

What toys do you have
in the bath?

Let's Explore introduces important concepts for
young children in a friendly and attractive way.

Bright, clear photographs stimulate discussion.

The simple, easy-to-read text incorporates
key words and sentence structures.

This book is a perfect starting point to
develop children's awareness of
babies and their needs.

Henry Pluckrose is a renowned educationalist
with a particular interest in developing
children's conceptual and inquiry skills.

Babies

Henry Pluckrose   WATTS

There's time for a bedtime story.
Then you say goodnight
and snuggle down to sleep.

Then it's morning and a new day!
No school – it's Saturday.
What will you do
with your time today?

Index

First published in 2000 by
Franklin Watts
96 Leonard Street
London
EC2A 4XD

Franklin Watts Australia
14 Mars Road
Lane Cove
NSW 2066

Copyright © Franklin Watts 2000

ISBN 0 7496 3658 0

Dewey Decimal
Classification Number 529

A CIP catalogue record for this book is
available from the British Library

Series editor: Louise John
Series designer: Jason Anscomb

Printed in Hong Kong

Picture Credits:
Steve Shott Photography, cover and title
page, pp. 9, 10, 12, 28, 31 plus all clock
photography; Ray Moller Photography p. 4;
Image Bank p. 24 (Elyse Lewin); Bubbles
p. 20 (Ian West); Eye Ubiquitous p. 6 (Roger
Chester), 27 (Kevin Wilton); Tony Stone
Images p. 17 (Andrew Olney); John
Walmsey Photography p. 23; Franklin Watts
stock photography pp. 15, 19.
With thanks to our models:
David Kimberley, José Ballesteros, Victoria
Harris and Sam Stephenson.